Everything You Need to Know About *Growth Spurts and Delayed Growth*

The adolescent years can be confusing and frustrating to many young adults, but the awkward feelings experienced by most teens eventually disappear.

Everything You Need to Know About Growth Spurts and Delayed Growth

Lesli J. Favor, Ph.D.

The Rosen Publishing Group, Inc.
New York

To the women in my family who helped me survive my puberty: my mom, Linda Frost; my sister, Jennifer Kniffin; and my grandmother, June Anderson

Published in 2002 by The Rosen Publishing Group, Inc.
29 East 21st Street, New York, NY 10010

Library of Congress Cataloging-in-Publication Data

Favor, Lesli J.
Everything you need to know about growth spurts and delayed growth / by Lesli J. Favor.
p. cm. — (The need to know library)
Summary: Outlines routine physical and emotional changes that are typical of any period of adolescence for both male and female children.
ISBN 0-8239-3549-3
1. Puberty—Juvenile literature. [1. Puberty. 2. Adolescence. 3. Growth.] I. Title. II. Series.
QP84.4 .F38 2002
612.6'61—dc21

2001005797

Manufactured in the United States of America

Contents

Introduction

If you could pick one word to describe the years between the ages of ten and twenty, what would it be? Some of the words often suggested by young people include the following: frustrating, exciting, scary, confusing, funny, embarrassing, painful, and powerful.

There is still another word that accurately describes exactly what changes young people experience during those mysterious, mostly fun, and sometimes frightening years. This word is puberty. You probably have a few ideas about what puberty is all about, such as understanding that your body gets taller and changes shape, and your emotional and sexual characteristics develop. To many young people, however, these physical changes are just one aspect of puberty. Your emotions, responses, and experiences are all just as important during this time.

Most teenagers are confused about this period in their lives, especially when they see and hear conflicting information in magazines and on television. Photographs and moving images of models and actors may make you feel as if your own body is not normal, when in fact it is the people in magazines and on television who are abnormal—that is, not average.

For example, when most teenage girls are asked what they'd like to change about their bodies, most will say, "I want to be thinner." They look at ultrathin models and skinny actresses and decide that, in order for them to be as beautiful, they must be as thin. Most girls do not know that in reality, the average adult woman is around five feet four inches tall and weighs about 140 pounds. In contrast, the average model is seven inches taller and more than twenty pounds lighter.

The media (the combined industries of television, commercial film, and publishing) causes teenage boys to struggle with their body image as well. During puberty, teenage boys begin to develop muscles and body hair. This hair is darker in color than the fine hair that is normally on their bodies and grows in the areas of the chest, back, legs, and groin. At some point, they will also have a growth spurt and quickly grow taller. Unfortunately, young men are confronted with images of impossibly buff and "perfectly" shaped men with glistening, hairless chests, strutting confidently in

Your peers and the media can influence how you feel about yourself and your role in society.

movies, commercials, and magazines. A young man can feel devastated and hopeless when he compares his own growing body to those he sees in the media.

When you consider that the average young person watches about three hours of television a day, and that nearly two-thirds of children and teenagers between the ages of eight and eighteen have televisions in their bedrooms, it's easy to understand this problem. When the media presents these impossible standards to young people, they react with equal amounts of doubt and confusion about how they view their own bodies.

As if the influence of the media was not difficult enough, your peers affect your body image and self-esteem, too. If you are taller than everyone else, for instance, you may try to hunch down to make yourself seem shorter and closer to everyone else's height. If you weigh more or less than your friends, you may be tempted to go on extreme diets to look more like them.

Yet another problem for both children and teenagers occurs when their peers tease them and mock their appearance. Young people can be quite cruel to one another—negative behavior that is endured by most people during the time when they are growing from a child to an adult. Sometimes, hearing continued taunting, laughter, or criticism feels like a nightmare you can't escape.

That's where this book may be helpful. Consider the information between these covers as your own personal survival guide. Are you wondering when you'll finally get taller? Have you been teased or bullied about your size or appearance? Have all your friends entered puberty, but your body is insisting on staying child-sized a little longer? Are you afraid you might have a medical condition that is keeping you from reaching puberty? You can find information on these topics and many others within the pages of this book.

Chapter 1

What to Expect During Puberty

The most important aspect to remember about adolescence is that your growth period during this time is very individualistic. People are each very unique and beautiful *because* they are all different.

Sarah plays volleyball each year for her school team. As usual, she has come in for her physical exam before the season starts. Dr. Ruiz tells Sarah that she has grown three inches and has gained twenty pounds since her physical a year ago.

"Is that normal?" she asks.

Everyone matures in his or her own unique way. You may be developing faster or slower than your friends, but you should not feel troubled about it.

"It's perfectly normal," says Dr. Ruiz. "You are going through a growth spurt, and it happens to everyone. Don't be surprised if you grow a little bit taller this year. You will probably gain a little more weight, too, as your breasts and hips develop."

"Oh, this is just great," Paul thinks to himself. "It's happening again."

"It" is an unexpected erection. Paul's body seems to be doing this a lot lately, and right now couldn't be worse timing. He is standing in front of the class, about to read his report on a scientific experiment. Luckily, he has worn loose-fitting pants. The bulge behind the fabric is unnoticeable to the class, but it is making him extremely uncomfortable.

Lately Paul has been feeling like a science experiment himself. Not only has he been getting erections and having wet dreams, but his voice cracks right in the middle of a word, and he has noticed that his body is producing new odors that he never noticed before—B.O., the guys call it—after a game of basketball.

"Has my body been taken over by aliens?" he wonders. "Will I ever be normal again?"

Sarah and Paul have something in common. They are both going through changes that young people experience during puberty.

You may think puberty is a word that seems custom-made to inspire jokes or giggles. How could a strange word like that be the name of an experience that is normal? In fact, most young people entering puberty wonder if they are normal. They may be confused or overwhelmed by all the changes that happen to their bodies.

What Is Puberty?

Puberty is the period of time when your body changes from a child's body into an adult's body. These changes take place over several years, so your body has some time to adjust physically and emotionally as you grow. Most girls begin puberty when they are between the ages of nine and twelve, and most boys begin this stage of life when they are between the ages of eleven and fourteen. It is important to remember, however, that everyone's growth happens on his or her own timetable. It is perfectly normal for you to enter puberty at one age and for your friends to develop sooner or later than you do.

The following chart distinguishes the changes you can expect during this rapid growth period.

Changes That Girls and Boys Have in Common

Growth Spurt: A period of rapid growth, when a girl's height may shoot up several inches and a boy's height may shoot up half a foot or more.

Weight Spurt: A time of weight gain when muscles develop and body fat is redistributed.

Pimples and Acne: Skin blemishes caused by the increased production of oil by glands beneath the skin's surface.

Body Odor: The strong smell associated with increased production of sweat. (Actually, it is the bacteria that feed on the sweat that cause the odor.)

Emotions: Sudden emotional feelings that swing from high to low.

Girls

Hair: Increased and possibly darkened body hair and pubic hair. Facial hair may also occur on some girls.

Breasts: Development of breast buds and then fully developed breasts; darkening of the breast nipples.

Menstruation: The monthly cycle of blood flow that discharges from the uterus through the vaginal opening.

Body Shape: Wider, more rounded hips and thighs; more rounded shoulders and breasts.

Boys

Hair: Increased and possibly darkened body hair, pubic hair, and facial hair.

Erections: Blood flow to the penis enlarges and stiffens it. Erections may occur unexpectedly and beyond your control. Erections may also occur during the night while you are sleeping.

Wet Dreams: Discharge of semen from the penis during an erection while asleep.

Voice: Deepening of voice.

Body Shape: Broader shoulders, more developed muscles, and a bulkier body.

What Will Happen During Puberty?

Girls and boys experience many of the same changes during puberty. One of the most noticeable changes is the growth spurt. A growth spurt is a burst of growth in height and overall body weight during a period of two to three years. If you are a girl, you may grow about three inches during this time; however, some girls grow more and some grow less. If you are a boy, you may grow about eight inches during a typical growth spurt. Some boys grow only half this much, while others may grow a full foot. After the rapid growth tapers off, you may still grow a little bit taller, especially if you are a boy.

Along with your increase in height, you will experience an increase in weight. It is not uncommon for a girl to gain from ten to thirty pounds during puberty. A boy may gain as much as twenty-five pounds during the year of his most rapid growth. By the time you reach age eighteen, you may weigh twice what you weighed at age ten!

What is the reason for this weight gain? Part is due to your added height. In addition, your body fills out into a more adult shape and size. If you are a girl, you will add muscle and fat in areas that give you a womanly shape. Your hips will become wider, your breasts will grow larger, and your shoulders will become rounder. If you are a boy, you will add a good deal of muscle as your body takes the shape of a man. You will continue to fill out, or gain bulk, until well into your twenties.

Hormonal changes that occur during puberty may cause skin blemishes due to an increase in oil secretions from glands.

Girls and boys also experience changes in skin tone, texture, and feel. Your skin will become oilier, and you may have pimples or acne on your face, chest, or back. Your skin will also sweat more and produce an adult body odor. Like all the other changes you experience during puberty, the stronger odor is caused by hormones. These hormones activate the special sweat glands under your arms, around your genitals, and in other places. This sweat contains chemicals that bacteria feed on, and these bacteria cause the odor. If you bathe regularly, especially after sports and other exercise, you will help keep this odor under control. You may also find deodorants and antiperspirants helpful.

Leave Me Alone!

In addition to these physical changes, young girls and boys will notice changes in their emotions during puberty. Have you ever felt happy one moment and then sad the next? Or have you felt very angry and then somehow amused? It is normal to experience a wide range of emotions, and it is even normal to be sad and depressed sometimes. After all, your body is going through tremendous changes, and you may sometimes feel like it is out of your control. Don't hesitate to talk to your friends who are experiencing the same changes. Friends can be a strong source of moral support, as can family members. If you feel overwhelmed or frightened by your emotions, you should talk to an adult you trust. You might also want to check out the Where to Go for Help section in the back of this book. Remember, you are not in this alone!

In addition to the changes that boys and girls both experience, there are some changes that are unique to girls and others that are unique to boys. First, let's take a look at some of the changes girls should expect.

Girls

If you are a girl, one of your earliest signs of puberty is breast buds. The word "bud" may make you think of a flower before it has bloomed. No, a girl's breasts are not flowers! But your breasts grow in the same way as a flower, beginning as small buds and growing over time to become fully formed. First, the nipples grow, and the skin around the nipples becomes darker. Then, the body begins to store more fat in the breasts, and your breasts grow larger. At times during their development, your breasts and nipples may feel especially tender. Occasionally, girls notice that one breast develops sooner than the other breast. This is actually quite normal and not at all alarming or a reason to worry.

Around the age of ten or eleven, you will notice pubic hair beginning to grow on the vulva, the area between your legs. The hair that develops there is sparse at first, but it will gradually grow much thicker. It may also spread outward toward the legs and upward toward the navel. In addition, hair grows in the armpits, and hair on the legs becomes thicker, more coarse, and darker. The hair on your arms may become thicker or darker, too. Some girls also grow hair on their upper lips, chins, or cheeks. This hair is normally fine (thin). Girls may also grow hair around their nipples and in the area between their breasts. Other girls do not grow this hair.

Whether you grow hair in all of these areas is due in part to heredity—if your mother or sisters grew hair in a certain area, you probably will, too. It's important to remember that there is a wide range of "normal" hair growth, and you and your friends will probably have slightly different types of hair growth during puberty.

Just as other changes during puberty vary from person to person, your body shape will be different from your friends'. Your hips will widen, but some girls' hips widen more than others girls'. Have you ever wondered why girls' hips tend to be wider than boys' hips? The widening of the hips in pubescent girls and young women allows more room for them to carry and deliver a baby.

Menstruation

In addition to all of these changes, you will also begin to menstruate. You may have heard menstruation called a "period." This is because a period is a monthly cycle. First, your uterus prepares a special, blood-rich lining in case you become pregnant. This special lining that is in your uterus will provide nutrients to an unborn fetus, should a fertilized egg begin to grow there.

If you are not pregnant, then during menstruation the uterus releases this blood-rich lining (blood and some body tissue), which trickles out of the vagina for a period of a few days to a week. The sight of the blood may startle you, but be assured that it is harmless, and your body quickly makes more blood to replace it. Ninety-five percent of girls get their first periods between the ages of nine and sixteen.

Boys going through puberty begin to experience hair growth and may decide to start shaving.

Boys

Among the types of changes you can expect as a boy are hair growth (called pubic hair) between your legs and around the base of your penis. You will also notice that the hair on your legs becomes thicker and darker, and hair grows in your armpits. Hair might also grow on your chest, shoulders, back, arms, stomach, and even your buttocks, but not all boys grow hair in these areas.

You will also begin to grow facial hair, usually by the time you are around the age of fifteen. However, some boys notice facial hair as early as fourteen, or as late as sixteen years of age. You should not worry if you haven't begun to grow a mustache or beard by age fifteen or sixteen, however. The first facial hair is usually lighter and thinner than it will become as you age. First, hairs will begin to grow at the outer corners of your mouth and will gradually fill in to form a complete mustache. Your sideburns and beard will begin as thin, light-colored hairs and will get darker and thicker as you age. Just as your body will continue to fill out in your early twenties, your facial hair may grow thicker during this time as well.

You will experience other changes, too. For one thing, your chest will fill out, and your shoulders will broaden. You will develop muscles, which add bulk and weight to your body. Your voice box, called the larynx, grows bigger, resulting in a deeper voice. Many boys go through a time when their voice tends to crack unexpectedly when they are speaking, usually around the age of fourteen or fifteen. Although you may feel embarrassed when your voice cracks, rest assured that you are perfectly normal, and your voice will soon stabilize. Right now, your vocal cords are growing longer and thicker, which is how your voice deepens. In fact, a boy's vocal cords will grow to about three times the length of a girl's vocal cords.

Most boys know that puberty is a time when sexual organs develop. Your penis and testicles will grow larger as a result of an increase in the body's production of the male hormone testosterone. Don't worry if you think your penis or testicles are not the same size as other boys'. These body parts come in many sizes, and they develop at different times. It is also normal for one testicle to be slightly larger than the other one. The size of the penis varies from person to person, too. By the end of puberty, most boys' penises are around two to four inches long when flaccid (soft) and around five to six inches long when erect. Still, variations in these sizes are normal and never affect the function of the penis.

You may have already heard of erections and wet dreams. Testosterone, which causes the development of the penis, sometimes causes it to fill with blood. The penis becomes stiff, making the penis stand out from the body in an erect position. This is why we use the word "erection."

It is not uncommon to get an erection even when you are not thinking about sex. In fact, young boys and babies sometimes get small erections. Sometimes these unexpected erections happen when you wake up in the morning, or you might get an erection during school hours. This situation can be very embarrassing. Still, you shouldn't worry since this is a common part of growing and it happens to all boys. The erection will probably not be noticed by others, even those standing or sitting nearby. Even so, you can do things such as holding a notebook in front of you, putting your hand in a front pocket, or wearing baggy pants or a long shirt to conceal this when it occurs. Concentrate on something else entirely, and the erection will go away on its own.

Every boy experiences wet dreams, too. Not only do you get erections when you are asleep, but you can also ejaculate while sleeping. This occurrence is called a wet dream because the penis ejaculates a small amount of semen (about a teaspoon), which causes a wet spot on your pajamas or sheets. After a wet dream, you may remember that you had a good dream, or you may not remember having had any dream at all. Either experience is a normal one.

For both girls and boys, puberty can last from a couple of years to five years or more. During this time, each person goes through changes at his or her own pace. In most cases, girls begin puberty several years before boys. However, some people are "late bloomers," which means they begin puberty later than most boys or girls their own age. You can find out more about delayed puberty in the next two chapters.

Chapter 2

I'm Not Like Other Girls

Martina was so embarrassed that she wanted to sink into the floor of the department store. Her mom stood in front of her, dangling a training bra from one finger. "Here, honey," her mom had just said loudly, "I think this is the smallest size they have."

But that wasn't the worst part.

Two guys she knew from school were walking by at just that moment. One of them glanced sideways after her mom spoke, caught sight of Martina's red face, and wiggled his eyebrows while grinning. She just knew he would tell everyone: Martina still wears "training" bras.

What Makes Me Different?

When your friends have already started to develop breasts, grow taller, or have their periods, you may feel left out or confused because you haven't experienced these changes yet. First of all, you should know that there is no single "correct" time to begin puberty. Just because you haven't grown breasts or started your period doesn't mean there is something medically or emotionally wrong with you. It also doesn't mean these changes will never happen! As hard as waiting is, this is just what you need to do for a while. Normally, girls who begin blooming later in life catch up by the age of sixteen. In the meantime, learn as much as you can about what you should expect during this time. On one hand, you may find it helpful to speak with your friends or a trusted adult about what you're feeling. On the other hand, you may not want to talk about it at all, and that's ok, too. Writing about your feelings in a private journal may make you feel better when you don't feel like talking.

Why Are My Breasts So Small?

Many girls feel very self-conscious if they have a flat or small chest. They may look at their friends' breasts and notice that their own breast development is lagging behind in comparison. Or they may see fashion models

A pubescent girl may feel self-conscious about having small breasts.

and actors in magazines, on television, and in movies who have fully developed bodies and wonder why their own breasts haven't developed. Worse, girls who haven't developed breasts yet may be teased by other girls, or even by boys.

What is a girl to do?

Some girls feel better when they are armed with knowledge about their bodies. Knowing what to expect doesn't make breasts grow, but it can keep your fears from taking over. The good news is that when you begin the stage of life known as puberty, your breasts are usually the first part of your body to begin changing. As you learned in chapter 1, you will grow breast buds first, and then they will fill out over time into fully developed, rounded, and shapely breasts that are the appropriate size for your individual body.

One thing to consider when waiting for breast buds to appear, or when waiting for those buds to fill out, is that breasts are composed largely of fat. Therefore, your diet plays a large part in breast development. This doesn't mean you need to eat large amounts of fatty foods to get breasts, but it does mean you need to eat nutritional foods and allow yourself to gain weight naturally as your body changes.

When you develop breasts is due in part to your genes. Ask other women in your family how old they were when they began to develop. The timing of your development is likely to be similar to theirs. In addition, these female family members can tell you how they dealt with the difficulty of lagging behind others in breast development. There is no need for concern unless breast buds haven't appeared by the age of fifteen.

Will I Always Be Short?

The average girl begins her growth spurt some time around the age of nine or ten years of age. But what if you are not average? If you are still short with a child's body shape when your friends are becoming tall and shapely, you may feel sad, depressed, or even angry. Some girls fear that they will be stuck at their short height forever.

Being shorter or taller than your friends is no cause for alarm, as everyone grows and matures at his or her own rate.

Knowing that your growth spurt is sure to come does not always help you feel better about your current size, or even your shape. What can you do while you twiddle your thumbs, waiting for that growth spurt to finally happen? First, you can pinpoint exactly what you do not like about being shorter than other girls your age. Do you want to appear sophisticated rather than cute? Would you like to be seen as someone who is a leader? Or do you want to feel more like one of the gang, when everyone in the gang is taller?

After you decide what irritates you about your height, you can take steps to feel better, making your size less of a problem. If you want to appear more sophisticated, carefully choose styles of clothing or hairstyles that are a bit more mature than you would normally choose. If people treat you as someone who is always babyish, respond in a mature manner. This will help them break the habit of seeing you as simply cute. If your friends or classmates overlook you as a leader because of your short stature, make an effort to change their perception of you. Take the initiative to fill leadership roles whenever you have the opportunity, such as heading up the debate team or asking to be team captain of a sport that you enjoy. If people do something such as pat you on the head or try to lift you up because you are smaller than your friends, don't laugh about it. Instead, tell them clearly to stop; you can use a serious voice or humor to get your point across, whichever is your style. Finally, remember to relax. Being comfortable in your own skin goes a long way in helping others form positive perceptions of you.

When Will I Get My Period?

It would be nice to know exactly when you will get your period—sort of like making an appointment for an important event. Unfortunately, it's not that easy. The good news is that there are signs you can watch for that can tell you when your period is a year or two away. Your breasts usually begin developing before you get your period, and you will begin to grow pubic hair (the hair between your legs) approximately one or two years before you get your first period. Some girls occasionally have vaginal discharge anywhere from six months to two years before they begin menstruating. Also, a girl needs to weigh at least ninety-nine pounds in order to get her period. She also needs between 17 and 20 percent of that total weight to be body fat. For her periods to continue regularly, she needs around 22 percent body fat.

All girls do not get their first period at the same age. Some may get their first period at the age of nine, while other girls begin menstruating anywhere from the age of eleven to sixteen. Chances are that if your mother got her period early, you will get yours early, too. If your mother got her period later, say at the age of fif-teen, yours may come at around that age, too. A woman's ability to become pregnant and be a good mother does not depend on whether she gets her period early or late. In addition, for the first few months or even a year after your period begins, it may not come every month, and it may not be the same number of days each time. It takes time for your body to adjust to its own individual rhythms.

As much as you would like to take a magic pill to get your period, grow taller, or develop breasts, that isn't an option unless something is medically wrong with you. (You can read chapter 5 in this book to find out about medical conditions and other situations that can affect the onset of puberty.) It may help you to know that so-called late bloomers still develop. By the end of your teenage years, things will have sorted themselves out.

Chapter 3

I'm Not Like Other Guys

"Hey, Short Stack! How's the weather down there?"

Josh closed his locker, glancing up at Chris. "Whatever. Are you going to the game on Friday?"

Last year, Josh would have slammed his locker in disgust. After all, his name is not Short Stack. Nor is it Shrimp or Squirt or PeeWee, but he has been called all these names. The problem: He is shorter than everyone else in his class. Sometimes he squirms with embarrassment when a tall girl talks to him. Just once he would like to swagger down the hall like one of the tall guys, looking over everyone's head, or at least seeing everyone at eye level.

This year, however, Josh decided not to let teasing get to him; teasers didn't deserve the satisfaction, he reasoned. Now, whenever someone teases him about being short or about being small in certain private places, he responds with a neutral comment. Then, he changes the subject immediately. He can usually steer the conversation to more common ground. He has noticed that people pick on him much less now. He is still not happy about being smaller, but at least he feels some control over how he is treated.

Why Do Some Boys Begin Puberty Later Than Others?

If your body has not yet entered puberty, you probably have many questions. You may feel unsure of yourself when you look around and notice that other boys your age have already begun to grow taller, fill out with muscle tone, or grow facial hair.

It is true that some boys enter puberty sooner than others, sometimes years sooner. As you learned in chapter 1, most boys experience the first signs of puberty between the ages of eleven and fourteen. However, remember that these ages are simply guidelines. There is nothing wrong with you if your body begins changing later. Each boy's body is different, and it will develop at its own scheduled pace.

Your body's growth is not totally random. Several factors affect not only your rate of growth but how much you grow. These factors are described in the list below:

◎ **Heredity:** Your body's growth is somewhat determined by heredity, the inherited genetic characteristics that help contribute to your individual schedule for development. If you can, find out when other men in your family began their growth spurts. If you are worried about late development, it is possible that other men in your family experienced the same delay.

◎ **Health:** General health is also important to your body's growth and development. If you think you may have a health problem that is delaying your growth or development, you should definitely talk to a school physician or family doctor. You can begin by reading the information in chapter 5, which introduces several medical conditions that affect growth. Ultimately, anyone who feels that he or she has any sort of medical condition should consult a medical professional immediately.

◎ Nutrition: Eating habits are just as important to your body's growth as the other factors in this list. For example, when you grow taller, your bones actually grow longer. It is important to give your body the nutrients it needs, such as calcium and iron, to make these and other important changes.

◎ Individual variation: The "wild card" in the list of influences on your growth is your own uniqueness. Because you are unique, you may respond differently to any of the other factors in this list than other boys do.

Why Do Other Guys in the Locker Room Seem So Well Developed?

All boys wonder about the growth of their penis at some time or another. If you have not begun to see signs of puberty in your genital area, you may be wondering what to expect. You may wonder if your penis will ever grow any bigger. As with other developments during puberty, changes like those in the size of your body's sexual organs happen on your own personal timetable. There is no need to worry unless you reach the age of eighteen and have not gone through any puberty changes.

You may find it hard to accept that other boys have begun their growth spurts and grown taller than you.

You may be interested to learn that your genitals are one of the first parts of your body to begin changing during puberty. You will probably see changes in your testicles, scrotum, and penis before you begin to grow taller or grow facial hair. First, the testicles grow larger, and the skin of the scrotum darkens in color. Then, the penis grows longer, and after that it grows thicker. Even after a boy's genitals grow during puberty, there is a difference in size from man to man. Most penises, however, are near the same size when they become erect.

Keep all this information in mind if you suspect that you are a late bloomer. If you need or want to speak with a doctor about your concerns, you can be sure that this is a discussion that is routine for him or her. The doctor can provide you with useful information that will help you feel better about the individual timetable of your body's growth.

Why Am I Shorter Than My Peers?

You may have already figured it out: Girls begin their growth spurts approximately two years earlier than boys of the same age. When you are ten and eleven years of age, you may notice the girls around you suddenly shooting up past your height. You may find this surprising, or you may not care much.

You may also find it more difficult to accept when other boys begin their growth spurts and quickly grow taller Even if you are late starting puberty, you will probably start by the age of fourteen. Only 2 percent of boys in the United States do not begin puberty by this age. Still, it may seem that everyone is taller than you. In a culture that places an emphasis on sports such as basketball and football, short people can feel shunned. Taller boys have the advantage in basketball, you may reason, and heavier boys have the advantage in football. Even if you care nothing at all for sports, it may seem that your social life is affected by your lack of height.

It would be nice if you could will yourself to grow by an act of determination, but this is impossible. You can, however, take charge of your body in other ways. Decide what it is about being short that you don't like, and take steps to change the situation if you can. If you are worried about being smaller than many girls, for example, remember that some of them are late bloomers, too. Some girls are naturally short. You may feel good being around these girls. You can also spend extra time developing a hobby or a sport that you are good at, regardless of height. Singing, martial arts, painting, and swimming are just a few. For other ideas, you can read chapter 4 of this book.

Can I Take Hormones to Make Myself Develop Faster?

Throughout your childhood, your parents or doctor probably kept track of your physical development. If there has been no cause for concern yet, chances are that you are perfectly normal; therefore you do not need to take additional hormones to induce rapid growth. These hormones do exist, but only children whose bodies cannot produce enough growth hormones on their own receive these synthetic (man-made) hormones from a doctor. In fact, you can take some satisfaction in the fact that you don't need to take synthetic hormones. This means you are normal, and your body will grow on its own.

Chapter 4

I Like Myself— I Think

"I've been trying to lose ten pounds," says Angela. "I want to wear the same size jeans that I wore last year, before I hit my growth spurt. Every day, I try to eat a little less, but sometimes even a bite of food makes me feel fat."

"It's just not fair," says Oscar. "I work out every week. I do push-ups and I lift weighs, but I never see results. Why can't I look like the guys I see on television? It's no wonder no one likes me."

When girls begin to get rounder shoulders, hips, and thighs, and when they develop breasts, they gain weight. As a result, many girls worry about those pounds and begin seeing their bodies as enemies. Girls are not alone in their worries about body size. Boys are often pressured to have well-defined muscles, and they

Media images of thin or surgically altered women can make girls feel bad about their bodies, even if they are perfectly normal.

are admired for being tall rather than short. In addition, boys are pressured to achieve a near-impossible balance of being "bulked up" with muscle without being overweight.

Puberty brings many changes for every young person, whether they are early, average, or late bloomers. They become focused on the changes their bodies are going through, or they obsess about what they wish would happen—developing larger breasts, for example, or a more muscular frame. In addition, girls and boys notice the sexual changes in each other, and they may react with interest, surprise, confusion, or even deep uncertainty.

Many teens feel self-conscious about the changes they are experiencing. Going through puberty can make you feel like you're under a microscope.

You are not alone in your struggle to understand and accept a changing body while trying to fit in with other young people. Different people handle the challenges of their changing bodies in different ways, but everyone goes through difficult changes. Unfortunately, some young people develop a negative body image—that is, they dislike their bodies and focus only on what they see as its faults and weaknesses.

A negative body image affects your self-esteem. Young people who don't like their bodies often don't like themselves either. Someone with poor self-esteem finds it hard to see his or her own value as a person. Instead, he or she feels inadequate, inferior, stupid, or insecure.

Is Puberty a Fun-House Mirror?

Sometimes, going through puberty can make you feel as though you are walking through a hall of fun-house mirrors. One day you feel short, the next day you feel scrawny, and another day you feel as big as a circus elephant. Nervously you glance around at everyone else, but they all look normal to you. Or worse, you glance at a magazine or television, and the people you see seem absolutely perfect: ultrathin bodies with flawless skin and well-defined muscles.

The truth is, the changes of puberty can make you feel like you are not yourself, but some distorted version of yourself. After all, your body is changing drastically from year to year, and you may even notice changes from month to month or from week to week. It is difficult to pinpoint exactly what you will feel like or look like because everything is continually evolving. And, in addition, you can't control what part of your body changes or when those changes will take place.

If Teasing Is So Funny, Then Why Am I Not Laughing?

"Hey, Beanpole, can you see my house from up there?"

"You can stand up now. Oh, you are standing up."

43

"They say you are what you eat. That must be why Ryan's face looks like a pepperoni pizza—red spots everywhere."

Teasing. It's just good, clean fun, right? Hardly. Anyone who has been teased can tell you that while everyone else stands around laughing, at least one person—the one who is being teased—feels hollow inside. He or she may force a laugh, but the truth is, teasing can cut deeply. Going through puberty—or waiting to begin puberty when all of your friends have started to grow up—can be an especially traumatic time. And teasing doesn't help.

Why do people tease each other? Often, those who tease are acting out of insecurity or uncertainty. They tease others about the very issue that bothers them most about themselves. Sometimes, teasing is done out of a desire to have power or control over others. Do any of these examples sound familiar?

◎ A boy who feels intimidated by another boy's tall height calls him "Frog Legs."

◎ A girl who worries about her own weight is quick to call others "Chubs" or "Cow."

◎ A boy jokes that someone else's penis is small so he can make everyone think his is larger.

Tips for Dealing with Teasing

- Showing anger or annoyance can encourage the person to tease you again because he or she enjoys getting a reaction from you. Instead, respond with a short, emotionless statement like "Nice," "Yeah," or "Whatever."

- Practice facial expressions that show you are not affected by teasing. For example, raised eyebrows with a tiny smile shows an expression of detached amusement. Slightly frowning (lowering eyebrows) while wrinkling your forehead shows a bit of disdain, which can be softened. Try these expressions! Forming a certain facial expression can cause you to feel the emotion related to that expression.

- Or don't respond to the teasing at all. Instead, walk away.

- Take note of people who often tease you. Choose not to spend time around them. Remember that you do not owe a teaser anything—not a response, not an explanation, and *not* your friendship.

Tips on Surviving Puberty

◎ Seek out sports or other physical activities that are suited to your height and interests. Short people may enjoy soccer, swimming, jogging, gymnastics, wrestling, and hockey. Tall people may want to try basketball, track, football, boxing, baseball, softball, and rowing.

◎ Find a hobby that has nothing to do with your height or size. Playing a musical instrument may appeal to you, or studying drawing, photography, or astronomy. You may enjoy baby-sitting or gardening. You might also like designing Web sites or writing songs, stories, or poems. If you run out of ideas, look through the yellow pages in the telephone book for things to learn or do.

◎ Keep a journal. Record how you are feeling from day to day. If you're not good with words, draw pictures of how you feel or use colors to show your emotions. Most people feel better about a problem after they've expressed themselves.

- Begin your own file of health records. Keep track of things like your height, weight, exercise schedule, and (for girls) menstrual cycle. Collect articles for your file that explain the changes your body goes through during puberty. This information will help keep you focused on realistic, healthy goals for your body, not impossible ideals from magazines or television.

What can you do if someone teases you? The most important reaction you can have is one of not caring. In a way, you are saying, "I do not give you permission to make me feel bad about myself. I'm worth more than that." You might also find some of the suggestions in the preceding boxes helpful.

How Can I Survive Puberty?

At this point, you may be filled with questions, such as, How can I adjust to my new height? How can I accept the added weight that comes with this adult body? How can I develop a better body image?

Don't worry, you can handle it. You've taken the first step by reading this book. Finding out what to expect and what is normal can chase away some of your fears. Knowing that everyone deals with his or her own body issues, whether the person shows it or not, helps you feel less isolated.

As you learned earlier in this book, the changes that come with puberty will probably happen to you sometime between the ages of nine and sixteen if you are a girl, or the ages of eleven and eighteen if you are a boy. The information you have read in this chapter may now help you adjust to these changes. In the next chapter, you can find out how nutrition, exercise, drugs, and medical conditions can also affect your development.

Chapter 5

This Isn't Supposed to Happen!

In order to grow and mature properly, your body must be healthy. The foods you eat and whether or not you exercise directly affect your body's growth. For example, muscles that are exercised grow stronger and larger than muscles that are not worked. Even your bones will grow stronger if you exercise.

A number of medical conditions can delay or stop growth or development, and this chapter will give you an overview of a few of them. If you believe your puberty is delayed or stopped as a result of any of these influences, you should talk to a doctor about it immediately. He or she can help you figure out what to do in order to help your body develop as it should.

Eating Disorders

Eating disorders include anorexia nervosa (often simply called anorexia) and bulimia, sometimes called "bingeing and purging." Any eating disorder can have serious and lasting effects on your growth and health. Eating disorders are not just a "girl thing." Boys can suffer from anorexia and bulimia, too. In fact, the number of boys with eating disorders is increasing. To find out how to get help for an eating disorder, you can talk to a doctor or look in the Where to Go for Help section of this book.

Anorexia Nervosa

A person who is anorexic severely limits the amount of food he or she eats. Anorexics starve themselves until they are dangerously thin and malnourished, yet they look in the mirror and still see their bodies as overweight. An anorexic may lose so much weight that he or she needs to be hospitalized and fed through tubes or needles. Some anorexics seek help too late to save their lives. Anorexia kills around 20 percent of those who suffer from it.

Bulimia

A person who is bulimic vomits all or most of the food that he or she eats or takes laxatives to force the body to get rid of the food through frequent bowel movements. Sometimes, bulimics eat huge amounts of food

Girls and boys who have a poor self-image and lack self-esteem sometimes develop eating disorders such as anorexia or bulimia.

and then throw it up. Like anorexics, bulimics see themselves as overweight whether they are or not. Most bulimics, however, appear fairly average in size. Bulimia, like anorexia, is life threatening. In addition, the frequent vomiting can cause problems with the teeth, stomach, bowels, heart, and circulatory system.

Exercise

Exercise is a good thing, right? Yes, but have you heard the phrase "too much of a good thing"? It is possible to exercise too much or to exercise improperly, affecting the body's ability to grow and develop.

Take weight lifting, for example. During puberty, your muscles go through a growth spurt along with your bones. Young people who haven't reached puberty may be tempted to lift weights to gain bigger, broader muscles. The truth is, before you enter puberty, your body does not produce enough of the hormones needed to grow bigger, stronger muscles. More important, however, you could actually damage your bones by lifting heavy weights before your body is ready. Since your bones don't completely harden until you finish puberty, the ends of your bones are still somewhat soft before puberty.

A good balance of exercise and diet is important to a girl's menstrual cycle, too. If a girl exercises and diets so much that her body fat falls below about 22 percent, she can stop getting her period. She experiences what is called amenorrhea. Some professional athletes and others who train hard without maintaining enough body fat go through amenorrhea. If you resume healthy eating and exercise habits, your regular periods usually begin again.

Drugs

Drugs such as steroids, tobacco, alcohol, marijuana, and others have negative effects on your growth.

Steroids stop your normal growth. Steroids can also cause you to develop bad acne, headaches, dizziness, and nosebleeds. In addition, boys who use steroids may find that their testicles have shrunk and their breasts have enlarged. Later in life, someone who has used steroids may have a heart attack, cancer, baldness, and even mental problems.

Other drugs, even so-called recreational drugs, hurt you. Smoking tobacco or marijuana causes lung damage. Using marijuana also causes your body to produce less growth hormone and less sex hormone, so your height and sexual maturity are harmed. Alcohol causes your body to slow down, and it also causes a loss of essential vitamins and minerals that your bones need to grow properly.

Medical Conditions

Various medical conditions can affect your growth before and during puberty. In order to grow taller during puberty, your body must produce enough human growth hormone (HGH) to cause your bones to grow longer. If your body does not produce enough HGH, you will not begin your growth spurt. For this reason, it is important to keep track of your growth, even before puberty. If your body is not growing as it should, your doctor can prescribe injections of HGH so that it can grow. At the end of puberty, around the age of sixteen for girls and eighteen for boys, your body stops growing in response to HGH, and your growth spurt is over.

Thyroid Deficiency

If the pituitary gland, which produces hormones, doesn't send enough thyroid hormone to the thyroid gland in your neck, your body's growth will be affected. A doctor can prescribe thyroid hormone pills to a young person whose body does not produce enough thyroid hormone.

Scoliosis

Imagine the shape of the letter *S*. Now, imagine someone's spine curved into that shape. This curvature of the spine is called scoliosis, and it can affect girls or boys during their growth spurt. Scoliosis does not cause pain, but if it is not treated, the spinal cord can become permanently curved. A curved spine limits a person's physical activity. If you have scoliosis and you see your doctor soon enough, you can receive treatment so that the problem is corrected. Your doctor may prescribe exercise, a temporary brace, or even surgery.

Turner's Syndrome

A girl who has Turner's syndrome does not have ovaries, which produce the sex hormone that causes sexual growth during puberty. The girl will not reach sexual maturity and will remain at a short height unless her doctor prescribes hormone treatments for her.

Cystic Fibrosis

Cystic fibrosis, an inherited condition, causes girls to begin puberty around two years later than normal. The body produces a thick, sticky mucus, which interferes with digestion of food and with breathing. Cystic fibrosis is most common in children of European descent. It is much less common in African Americans, and it hardly ever occurs in Asians. Doctors treat cystic fibrosis with a combination of enzyme supplements, special diet, exercise, and antibiotics.

Keeping Things in Perspective

Going through puberty is difficult enough when you do not have a medical condition or other problem affecting your body's growth. Struggling with problems caused by diet, exercise, drugs, or a medical condition can seem like the last straw. Take heart! If you work closely with your doctor and are diligent about your eating and exercise habits, you can get help. Your situation will get better, and you won't have to go through it alone.

Glossary

amenorrhea Abnormal condition in which a female stops menstruating.

anorexia nervosa Eating disorder with symptoms including excessive weight loss, avoidance of food, extreme dieting, and obsessive exercise.

bulimia Eating disorder with symptoms including eating large amounts of food and then vomiting it up.

ejaculation Sudden secretion of semen from the penis.

erection Filling and stiffening of the penis with blood.

genitals Sexual and reproductive organs.

late bloomer Person who enters puberty later than average.

menstruation Monthly cycle in which a female's uterus sheds the lining it had prepared for the possibility of pregnancy.

mucus Thick, liquidlike bodily secretion that may be stretchy or sticky.

muscle Tissue in the body that is responsible for movement.

ovary Female reproductive gland that produces eggs.

penis Male sex organ and the organ through which urine is excreted.

period Informal word for menstruation.

puberty Period of time when the body matures and develops sexually.

pubic hair Hair that grows in the genital area.

scrotum Pouch of skin that holds the male's testicles.

semen Thick, white fluid containing sperm that the penis ejaculates.

testicles Two round sex glands that are in the male's scrotum.

uterus Hollow organ in the female in which a fetus grows during pregnancy.

vagina Stretchy canal-like opening between the uterus and the vulva in females.

vaginal discharge Mucus secreted from the vagina.

vulva External female genitals.

wet dream Ejaculation during sleep.

Where to Go for Help

Hotlines

National AIDS Hotline
(800) 342-AIDS

National Runaway Switchboard
(800) 621-4000

National STD Hotline
(800) 227-8922

National Youth Crisis Hotline
(800) 448-4663

Teen Suicide Hotline
(800) 522-8336

Organizations

Al-Anon/Alateen
1600 Corporate Landing Parkway
Virginia Beach, VA 23454-5617
(800) 356-9996
e-mail: wso@al-anon.org
Web site: http://www.al-anon.alateen.org

American Anorexia Bulimia Association (AABA)
165 West 46th Street, Suite 1108
New York, NY 10036
(212) 575-6200
Web site: http://www.aabainc.org

Boys & Girls Clubs of America
(800) 854-CLUB (2582)
Web site: http://www.bgca.org

National Association of Anorexia Nervosa and
        Associated Disorders (NAANAD)
P.O. Box 7
Highland Park, IL 60035
Hotline: (847) 831-3438
e-mail: info@anad.org
Web site: http://www.anad.org

National Council on Alcoholism and Drug Dependence
20 Exchange Place, Suite 2902
New York, NY 10015
(800) NCA-CALL
e-mail: national@ncadd.org
Web site: http://www.ncadd.org

National Mental Health Association (NMHA)
1021 Prince Street
Alexandria, VA 22314-2971
(703) 684-7722
Mental Health Information Center: (800) 969-NMHA
Web site: http://www.nmha.org

Web Sites

Adolescence Directory On Line (ADOL)
http://education.indiana.edu/cas/adol/adol.html

Drug Abuse Resistance Education (D.A.R.E.)
http://www.dare.com

Teen Health and the Media
http://www.teenhealthandthemedia.net *or*
http://depts.washington.edu/ecttp/default.html

For Further Reading

Blackstone, Margaret, and Elissa Haden Guest. *Girl Stuff: A Survival Guide to Growing Up*. San Diego: Gulliver Books, 2000.

Bode, Janet. *Food Fight: A Guide to Eating Disorders for Preteens and Their Parents.* New York: Simon and Schuster, 1997.

Bryan, Jenny. *Adolescence*. Austin, TX: Raintree/ Steck-Vaughn, 2000.

Cooke, Kaz. *Real Gorgeous: The Truth About Body and Beauty*. New York: W. W. Norton and Co., 1996.

Daldry, Jeremy. *The Teenage Guy's Survival Guide*. Boston: Little, Brown and Co., 1999.

Johnston, Marianne. *Let's Talk About Alcohol Abuse* (The Let's Talk About Library). New York: The Rosen Publishing Group, Inc., 1997.

Lewellen, Judie. *The Teen Body Book: A Guide to Your Changing Body*. Los Angeles: Lowell House Juvenile, 1999.

Madaras, Lynda, and Area Madaras. *My Body, My Self for Boys: The "What's Happening to My Body?" Workbook*. New York: Newmarket, 1995.

Madaras, Lynda, and Area Madaras. *My Body, My Self for Girls: The "What's Happening to My Body?" Workbook*. New York: Newmarket, 1995.

Index

About the Author

Lesli J. Favor is an author living in Dallas, Texas, where she spends her time writing for young people. She clearly remembers her own growth spurt in the fifth grade, when she was taller than all but two people in her class. Today, she stands a proud five feet two inches tall.

Photo Credits

Cover, pp. 2, 8, 11, 17, 21, 27, 29, 37, 41, 42 © Index Stock; p. 51 © Corbis.

Book Designer

Nelson Sá